for Lent 1997

A Page a Day

Pages contributed by
Sisters of Charity of Saint Elizabeth
Edited by Anita M. Constance, S.C.

Paulist Press
New York • Mahwah, N.J.

ISBN: 0-8091-3687-2

Illustrations contributed by Mary Culhane, S.C., and Frances Scarfone, S.C.

Published by Paulist Press
997 Macarthur Boulevard
Mahwah, New Jersey 07430

Printed and bound in the
United States of America

Spring speaks to our human nature, echoing the call to growth, new life and possibilities. The church assures us that God is faithful and with us in the process. Lent gives us the opportunity to take advantage of God's "good" nature, drawing us out of our old ways, freeing us from the fear that we will never change. Commitment and grace bond us to God, and in Jesus our hopes are fulfilled.

What binds us to God also binds us to one another. We cannot escape the truth that we have companions as we journey toward the light of Easter morning. This companionship brings responsibilities—for the kingdom of God is grounded in kinship. Upon this foundation, the church continues to be built; from the firmness of this womb, the church continues to be born. The church grows because we continue to grow.

The following pages are opportunities to seek the deeper recesses of our human nature, to find God at the center, and to discover the grace that companionship can bring.

—*Anita M. Constance, S.C.*
Editor

O loving Jesus, on this first day of Lent
please open my eyes to see,
my heart to feel, my soul to touch...you
in a special way today.
That, in you, I might become
the very holiness of God!
Powerful powerful powerful words, these!
How can I ever be as aware, as compassionate
as patient, as just, as you?
Ah, but you ask me to become...to struggle
toward...
to grasp this goal of holiness. Oh, still so
unattainable
unless, unless...ah, yes...in you, you say,
in you we might become that very holiness of God.
In you, O Lord, our Lent begins.
In you, O Lord, may life take on
the deeper hue of you!
May all that colored your earthly life...
your gentleness, your loving care,
discover me and take root there.
Amen!

Ash Wednesday, February 12

Readings: Joel 2:12–18; Psalms 51;
2 Corinthians 5:20–6:2; Matthew 6:1–6, 16–18

Choose life.

—Deuteronomy 30:19

One of the greatest of God's gifts to us is the freedom to choose. We are the only creatures on earth to have this ability. In the book of Deuteronomy, the Israelites were admonished to choose life, not death. The same message is addressed to us today. We, too, must choose life—to live content in God's love, trusting that God wants only good for us.

That seems easy enough to do, but in reality, it can be quite difficult at times. What prevents us—me—from choosing life? At times it is my fear of what God will ask of me. Other times it is my fear of having to change my lifestyle, having to give up control of life situations. Sometimes it is just laziness. It seems that whenever I put myself *before* God, it is then that I choose death.

Lord, help me be aware of your ever present grace as I struggle to change—to choose life.

Today I will try to be more aware of God's presence in my life and say yes to those invitations.

Readings: Deuteronomy 30:15–20; Psalms 1; Luke 9:22–25

The practice of fasting is a most powerful aid to prayer. Consistent fasting leads to a radical turning to God in deep interior prayer. Fasting enhances our God-like response to life; we can expect useful, spiritual results. We must consider fasting not only as an acceptance of physical pain so that we might know the sufferings of Jesus but also as an entrance into a state of awareness.

Jesus himself said, "Blessed are those who hunger and thirst for righteousness, for they will be filled" (Matthew 5:6). As the pangs of hunger attack us, our spirits are lifted. We no longer concentrate on being hungry for food but are moved to the very center of our being. There we find ourselves experiencing the prophecy given in Isaiah 58:8, "Then your light shall break forth like the dawn, and your healing shall spring up quickly; your vindicator shall go before you, the glory of the LORD shall be your rear guard."

Heavenly Father, may my fasting this Lent center me upon rejoicing in the great feast of Easter.

Readings: Isaiah 58:1–9a; Psalms 51; Matthew 9:14–15

I have come to call not the righteous but sinners to repentance. —Luke 5:32

Many of us go to great lengths to stay in good health. We eat the right foods, exercise, take vitamins—thus avoiding a trip to the doctor. Yet there are times when, despite all our efforts to stay well, our bodies warn us that something is amiss. Unless we see a doctor, serious illness can overtake us; so it is with our spiritual life. We pray, attend mass, receive the sacraments, yet we struggle with our weaknesses, trying again and again to overcome some fault. At times we are plagued with temptations. These may be warning signs that all is not well in our spiritual life.

Lent is a time for a spiritual check-up—to examine the shape of our spiritual well-being, our relationship with God. Jesus' words, today, can be a source of comfort to those of us seeking holiness—he is there for us in our struggle.

Let us not hesitate to call upon the Divine Physician for healing of body and soul:

> *Incline your ear, O LORD and answer me,*
> *for I am poor and needy.* —*Psalms 86:1*

Readings: **Isaiah 58:9–14; Psalms 86; Luke 5:27–32**

O my God, in you I trust.
—Psalms 25:2

Sometimes we get ourselves into a state of anxiety, worrying about situations we cannot control. We really feel alone. Often we ask, "Where is God?" The truth is that God is always with us. The church is the visible sign of that presence. Baptism and eucharist bring God's Spirit and life right within us, never to leave under any circumstances. We must remember this.

In times of trouble, we may want to pray in the manner of the psalms. There, our Hebrew brothers and sisters addressed God, first, to get God's attention. Then they reminded God of all the ways God delivered them from problems in the past. They asked God to pay attention to their current problems and to do the same—be as faithful—once again. At the end, they did a wonderful thing—they praised God and trusted that God would hear and answer them.

Today I pray: O my God, in you I trust!

Readings: Genesis 9:8–15; Psalms 25;
1 Peter 3:18–22; Mark 1:12–15

For I was hungry and you gave me food, I was thirsty and you gave me something to drink.

— Matthew 25:35

The hungers of the human family take many forms. Each hunger, each yearning is a gift from God. Gift, too, and instrument of God's mercy are all those people who feed the hungers and slake the thirsts of the human family:

> *the hunger for food*—fed by soup kitchens, farmers, parents, bakers, and fishermen;
> *the hunger for knowledge*—filled by teachers, scientists, librarians, and journalists;
> *the hunger for beauty*—nourished by artists, homemakers, architects, and gardeners;
> *the hunger for companionship*—eased by good neighbors, friends, and communities of faith;
> *the hunger for meaning*—unfolded by philosophers, holocaust survivors, theologians, and wisdom figures;
> *the hunger for justice*—mitigated by community organizers, employers who pay a just wage, and Madres de Plaza silently demanding information about the disappeared;
> *the hunger for tenderness*—soothed by hospice workers, therapists, and loving spouses.
>
> This is the work of God, and joy is found in the doing!

Today I ask what are my deepest hungers? How am I nourished? What does God reveal to me in both the yearning and the satisfaction?

Readings: Leviticus 19:1–2, 11–18; Psalms 19; Matthew 25:31–46

My hope is in you.

—Psalms 39:7

Isaiah reminds us that God's actions achieve what they intend. We can count on that as much as we can know that rain and snow will water the earth, making it fertile and fruitful. God's word comes to us in scripture, in liturgy, in the community, in nature, and in a unique and definitive way in the person of Jesus Christ. It is Jesus who reveals to us that our God is a loving Father.

Jesus calls us to pray daily, and in the Our Father he models for us how we are to pray. Jesus teaches us that our conversation with God is about praise, adoration, thanksgiving, and petition. Giving glory to God, acknowledging our dependence on God, praying for the coming of God's reign, asking for our daily bread—not only the bread that feeds us physically but also the bread that nourishes our very being—and asking for forgiveness, recognizing that this requires that we forgive those who have offended us. This is the stuff of our daily prayer!

How attentive am I to God's word? Today I will pray the seven petitions of the Our Father in a meditative way and respond with some concrete action.

Readings: Isaiah 55:10–11; Psalms 39; Matthew 6:7–15

Go to Nineveh, that great city, and proclaim to it
the message that I tell you.　　　　—Jonah 3:2

Like Jonah, I too am called to be a prophet—to
proclaim the word of God. Because I have
experienced God's love and mercy, the words
seem to come easily and others willingly listen.

The call to conversion from sin is more difficult
for me to articulate. I do see the evil around me
and I am aware of the sin in my own life, but I
hesitate to speak. Perhaps I fear being
considered "conservative" or "not with it."
Perhaps I am not a credible witness to the word I
speak.

*Loving God, I thank you for the privilege of
proclaiming your word. Today I beg you for the grace
to live what I proclaim.*

Readings: Jonah 3:1–10; Psalms 51;
Luke 11:29–32

Ask, and it will be given you; search, and you will find; knock, and the door will be opened for you.
— Matthew 7:7

Listening to these words gives me a wonderful image of God. A God who stands at the door and says, "Yes, I will give you what you ask. Yes, I will guide you in finding your way. Yes, my heart is always open to you. Just ask, seek, knock!"

I think of friends who tell me, "You are always welcome. My door is always open to you." What a comfort this is, even if I never need to go through their doors, or go there only infrequently. And should they ask, seek, or knock, I would be there for them too. Then I realize that God loves me even more than any human person; God is so loving that I find it hard to comprehend. And so I pray:

Here I am, O loving God.
I ask...I seek...I knock.
Grant me what I need this day.
Help me to seek only you.
Your open door beckons me.
Thank you for your love.

Readings: **Esther C:12, 14–16, 23–25;**
Psalms 138; Matthew 7:7–12

I wait for the LORD, my soul waits, and in his word I hope. —Psalms 130:5

Faith is a special gift from God. It is a gift that requires a response of trust. I say that I believe in God, but do I really trust him? Am I willing to put my hands into his wounded hands and go where he leads me?

For me, this capacity to trust was nurtured by the lessons of life. I learned a lot about trust from my parents, especially during the Depression. Their favorite prayer was, "God will provide," and God did! People responded by helping one another. Clothes and food were shared. My mother was always sure to make our dinner, simple as it was, stretch to include a little extra, just in case someone dropped in.

This is the trust God wants—faith come alive by sharing myself with others!

O Sacred Heart of Jesus, I place my trust in you.

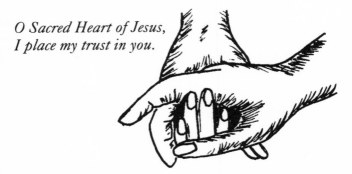

Readings: Ezekiel 18:21–28; Psalms 130; Matthew 5:20–26

He [Jesus] said to them, "But who do you say that I am?"
                                    —Matthew 16:15

I know so well, Lord, that this question is directed to me, just as it was to your disciples so many years ago. The world around me often ignores you or acts as if you are merely a historical figure whose teachings are not relevant to our times.

But who do *I* say that you are? You are my brother, my redeemer, my inspiration, my security—the center of my life. Do my actions give witness to this, or do they belie my words? Can others read my answer in the way that I live each day?

Like Peter, let me be a "rock" now on which you can build your church—your love—against which death itself has no power.

I will pause at least three times today—morning, noon, evening—to look at how I am giving answer to your question, "Who do you say that I am?"

Readings: 1 Peter 5:1–4; Psalms 23; Matthew 16:13–19

Take your son, your only son Issac…as a burnt offering…. I know that you fear God, since you have not withheld your son, your only son, from me.
—Genesis 22:2, 12

[God] did not withhold his own Son, but gave him up for all of us. —Romans 8:32

There came a voice, "This is my Son, the Beloved."
—Mark 9:7

There is a mounting poignancy as the phrase, "My son, my only son" is repeated throughout today's scripture passages. Abraham, who waited long and longingly for a son, is asked to kill him in sacrifice. What request could possibly be more demanding of anyone's trust and confidence? Only implicit faith and trust could have enabled Abraham's response. Then we read that God, who made this seemingly impossible request, did not withhold *his* only son. God gave Jesus up for us!

Abraham remembered that his only son, Isaac, was one of God's many gifts to him and answered, however agonizingly, with love, trust, and gratitude.

God's gift to us, who at times are unloving, undeserving, and ungrateful, is *freely* given because God *freely* loves. We have received God's son; what must be our response? Even if God asks for our "only son," that which is most dear to us, will we, like Abraham, gladly and trustingly say, "Yes"?

Readings: Genesis 22:1–2, 9a, 10–13, 15–18; Psalms 116; Romans 8:31b–34; Mark 9:2–10

Be merciful, just as your Father is merciful. Do not judge, and you will not be judged; do not condemn, and you will not be condemned. Forgive, and you will be forgiven.

—Luke 6:36–37

> I had a dream the other night
> With heaven as its theme.
> I saw God in this land of light
> And was astonished with the scene.
> I saw some folks whom I had judged
> And others I condemned.
> And had to face the bitter truth
> That I was not perfect in the end.

The voice of Jesus cries out strongly in this gospel passage and touches us in our daily life where the call to be loving is not only for the great and unique moments in life but, above all, for the ordinary times.

This Lenten passage challenges us to repent, reform our lives, and live the Good News. Its true spirit enables us to step out of ourselves and concentrate on others and God's inestimable love and compassion for us despite our failings.

Today I will practice loving, forgiving, giving. Today I will not condemn or judge another.

Readings: **Daniel 9:4b–10; Psalms 79; Luke 6:36–38**

They tie up heavy burdens, hard to bear, and lay them on the shoulders of others; but they themselves are unwilling to lift a finger to move them.
—Matthew 23:4

With a burst of energy and love, I enter today focusing on my potential to lift the burdens of others. Using the gifts of understanding and compassion, I assume my daily responsibilities. Who around me might be weighed down by the heat of the day? I am determined to lift not only a finger but a loving heart in full gospel response to free God's people.

O Jesus, give me your spirit to see others as you see them. Enable me to listen with the "ear of my heart." Move me to walk the extra mile with my brothers and sisters.

Today I will look between life's lines in others. I will select one small action to ease another's burden.

Readings: Isaiah 1:10, 16–20; Psalms 50; Matthew 23:1–12

And he [Jesus] said…, "What do you want?…Are you able to drink the cup that I am about to drink?" —Matthew 20:21–22

What is it you want? That is the kind of question that catches your ear, your eye, and your breath. If I am honest, I want a lot. I want material things, good health, and a host of other things: love, affirmation, satisfaction. The list is endless.

Certainly I would never want or choose to drink the cup that Jesus was about to drink, or any suffering for that matter. What Jesus offers is the mystery of the cross—the divine paradox.

O Jesus
focus me, lead me, guide me.
Teach me the meaning of suffering,
the validity of the cross.
Cross over into my life
the graces that I need
to accept redemptive suffering
daily, so I may walk in
your footsteps and live your love.

Readings: Jeremiah 18:18–20; Psalms 31; Matthew 20:17–20

But their delight is in the law of the LORD, and on his law they meditate day and night. They are like trees planted by streams of water, which yield their fruit in its season, and their leaves do not wither. In all that they do, they prosper.

—Psalms 1:2–3

Dear God, you know it is a great delight to follow some of your laws; you said yourself that some are hard. So I do struggle at times to live by your law because human nature—my nature—is prone to selfishness. You know, God, first, I come; then, I come; then, I come once more. You and my neighbor are at the end of the line too often.

Yet, you nourish me with your grace and support me by your presence. I am like the trees that you made sure were planted by streams of your abundant life. As they yield fruit, please enable me to share my fruitfulness with others—the fruit of peace, joy, and love that keeps our lives from withering on the vine when the ills of society surround and threaten us on every side.

May the prosperity I seek be the happiness you intend for me. These blessings will be mine if my heart beats with the rhythm of your loving heart. So be it, holy God!

Readings: Jeremiah 17:5–10; Psalms 1; Luke 16:19–31

Now Israel [Jacob] loved Joseph more than any other of his children. —Genesis 37:3

Joseph's brothers, enraged and resentful of their father's special love for him, were angry enough to sell or kill or do just about anything to rid themselves of their brother. Their anger and jealousy blinded them to the realization that Jacob was aging. Holding on to a young son made Jacob feel alive and hopeful. His love for his other sons did not diminish, but as long as Joseph was present, their anguish was relentless.

How often, in life's situations, one person can appear to be favored over others. Then it seems as if no one else matters or can do things quite as well. Some feel crushed in such a climate, turn inward, and become self-deprecating. It is then time to stop, take notice and recognize our gifts *for ourselves*, and not depend on others to affirm and support us.

We all must be willing to see value in a person, including ourselves, and recognize the myriad gifts each possesses. It is then that we can love even the "favored one."

Dear God, help me to recognize the gifts of those around me. Inspire me with the insight and appreciation of those who have different gifts than I. Help me to affirm them, even when I am tempted to be less than generous in my judgment.

Readings: **Genesis 37:3–4, 12–13a, 17b–28; Psalms 105; Matthew 21:33–43, 45–46**

When he had spent everything…he began to be in need. —Luke 15:14

There were three people:
- —One was greedy, foolish, envious, desperate, clever, and *quite* manipulative.
- —One was self-righteous, jealous, arrogant, angry, selfish, and *very* judgmental.
- —One was joyful, responsive, generous, understanding, compassionate, and *so* loving!

Who among us has not been all three? May I come to peace with *all* that is in me and be accepting of all that I am.

Today I will be grateful for all the responses, generosity, understanding, compassion and love that I have experienced.
I will reflect on what the day asks of me, perhaps
- —to return to someone's good graces
- —to speak the truth of my feelings
- —to extend myself to someone in need of any kind.

Bless the LORD, O my soul[!] —Psalm 103

Readings: Micah 7:14–15, 18-20; Psalms 103; Luke 15:11–32

With what joy does the word of God flood my soul today! I am so beloved that God wants me jealously. **"I the LORD your God am a jealous God,...showing steadfast love to...those who love me and keep my commandments"**

—Exodus 20:5–6

How do I view these commandments? Are they stern prohibitions of what I must not do, or rather, do I see them as safeguards, a protecting wall to prevent my human frailty from disappointing such a steadfast lover?

Saint Paul reminds us that Christ crucified is foolishness and a stumbling block to the unwise. But the wisdom and the power that support us are revealed in the precepts of the Lord, "rejoicing the heart." The psalmist joins with the heavens and the firmament proclaiming the perfection of the law of the Lord—to be desired more than "much fine gold."

I shall make time to ponder today's readings from scripture. I shall hear the words of God, not in fear and trembling as they were given to Moses, but with the joy that Christ brings when he asks me to be perfect as my heavenly Father is perfect.

March 2, Third Sunday of Lent

Readings: Exodus 20:1–17; Psalms 19; 1 Corinthians 1:22–25; John 2:13–25

As a deer longs for flowing streams, so my soul longs for you, O God. My soul thirsts for God, for the living God. —Psalms 42:1–2

O God, what is this ache, this desire, this longing that haunts me every so often? When I am engulfed in it, I analyze and conclude that perhaps it is a need for the companionship of a friend, or more enjoyment in life, or a different job, or better physical or mental health, or a more comfortable home.

At times I am seeking one or another of these things, yet I sense my heart's desire is more than this. For when you have fulfilled my requests, contentment and peace follow, but then the searching and longing begins again.

Still, you gently and lovingly keep granting me what I want. When will I live with conviction that you are all that I long for? You have formed me from Love—with and for Love. You are the living water that nourishes my being and gives life to my unfolding. You are my all!

May I drink today from the streams of your love with thanksgiving and share a cup with someone who thirsts as I.

Readings: 2 Kings 5:1–15a; Psalms 42; Luke 4:24–30

Make me to know your ways, O LORD.

—Psalms 25:4

Today's readings focus on Yahweh, the faithful one, who holds no grudges or debts against our omissions and commissions toward our neighbor. Instead, God calls us to a spirit of forgiveness.

Forgiveness is a process that frees us. It allows us to put to greater use the energy once consumed by our holding onto grudges, harboring resentments, and nursing unhealed wounds.

Forgiveness is recognizing the inner strength we always possessed that reaches into our limitless capacity to understand and forgive others in a true spirit of compassion. It is breaking through the cycle of blame, thereby ceasing to recreate new victims by hurting others as we have been hurt.

Today I will call to mind someone whom I need to forgive for some past hurt. I will pray with Psalm 25:17,

Relieve the troubles of my heart,
and bring me out of my distress.

Readings: Daniel 3:25, 34–43; Psalms 25; Matthew 18:21–35

Tuesday, March 4

Do not think that I have come to abolish the law or the prophets; I have come not to abolish but to fulfill. —Matthew 5:17

What did Jesus mean when he said, "fulfill"? Jesus came to bring to fruition the heart of the ten commandments, the foundation of the law: reverence, love, justice, and respect for God, the people of God, and God's creation.

Jesus came to model that love, that reverence, that respect. He demonstrated, by his life and his example, what it meant to live this way. Jesus showed that life was not to be bound up by "shoulds" and regulations but rather liberated by love, mercy, and forgiveness.

Today, we are invited to act more justly, to love more tenderly, and to walk more humbly with our God. Let us live each moment out of love, reverence, and respect.

Jesus, give me what I need today in order to fulfill what your law of love invites me to.

Readings: Deuteronomy 4:1, 5–9; Psalms 147; Matthew 5:17–19

Obey my voice, and I will be your God and you shall be my people.
—Jeremiah 7:23

Our God continually pursues us even in the midst of our disbelief, disinterest, or inability to recognize the power of a loving Creator in our lives. Today's readings lament these shortcomings but at the same time always hold the promise of relationship before us. We are prodded to be faithful and faith-filled, to listen to the word, to turn our face toward God, to "not harden your hearts" (Psalms 95).

The Lenten season is a time when we reflect on our attitudes and behaviors and critique them, especially in light of the call to be faithful. We are invited to open our hearts and to listen to God's voice.

Loving God, help me to be faithful in bringing your message of love to our world. God of all people, grace me with a heart open to those who are different than I. Persistent God, keep calling out to me as I seek to strengthen my resolve to hear your voice in the daily rhythm of life.

Readings: Jeremiah 7:23–28; Psalms 95; Luke 11:14–23

Thursday, March 6

Love the Lord your God.
…Love your neighbor as yourself.
—Mark 12:30–31

Teach me your ways, O Lord.

I sing to the Spirit of Wisdom...
  Take it to heart. Me? Take what to heart?
  Love. Sure I love—I love everybody.
What? Do I understand what is written? Like
love means promoting justice? You mean I
cannot have peace unless all are fed with the
finest of wheat? But...
I love. I love the colors of life and the rhythm of
spring.
I love. I feel. I reach out.…
I touch the beauty of people and I am touched.
I reach for another and I am embraced.

I cannot be fed alone, you say.
Together, we will eat. Together, we will love.
Together, we will sing a new song to Wisdom.
Come.
Together...Come!

**_Readings:_ Hosea 14:2–10; Psalms 81;
Mark 12:28b–34**

Have mercy on me, O God, according to your steadfast love; according to your abundant mercy blot out my transgressions. —Psalms 51:1

How many times through the years have I prayed these words and begged for God's mercy and forgiveness? In today's gospel narrative, Luke presents the story of the Pharisee and the tax collector. I know that I too am called to confront my own complacency and self-adulation and to beg God's mercy once again.

Forgiving God, you continually call me to repentance, to true sorrow for my sins, to renewed efforts to overcome my weaknesses. Now, this Lent, your divine urgency draws me closer—to believe in your love, your personal love for me. It is only by believing in your love and forgiveness that I can leave the past behind and grow in intimacy with you.

With this hope, I pray, too, for the grace to reach out with forgiveness to others—to live that life of compassion that you have shared with me. Amen.

Readings: **Hosea 6:1–6; Psalms 51; Luke 18:9–14**

Christ, God's eternal gift of life, leaves us not a legacy of wealth in earthly riches but an inheritance of spirit and will, heart and mind. For we have been transformed in this earthly life because of "the immeasurable riches of his grace in kindness toward us in Christ Jesus"

—Ephesians 2:7

We are what we are only through God's mercy as revealed in the suffering and death of the Word-made-flesh of God. In and through Jesus Christ we are! *This* is our life! *This* is our legacy!

I will recite my favorite prayer today, remembering my purpose the first time I prayed it—the "life" it won for me or others. Then I will thank my Savior for the graces I received.

Readings: 2 Chronicles 36:14–17, 19–23; Psalms 137; Ephesians 2:4–10; John 3:14–21

For I am about to create new heavens and a new earth; the former things shall not be remembered.   —Isaiah 65:17

What perfect readings for the middle of Lent! The approach of Easter is also the approach of spring and signs of the new earth (new life, new light, new warmth) that spring heralds. The winds of March cleanse the trees of old dead branches, leaving breathing space for the budding of new growth. The snow and the rain of late winter prepare the hard ground for the new growth of spring.

It's not hard to see the parallel between the new earth and the newness the Lord promises to create within us. Our longing for the fulfillment of Easter is growing stronger—off with the old, on with the new!

The first reading encourages me to make some trade-offs—dancing for mourning, gladness for sackcloth, music for silence, new for old, life for death. *So if it pleases you, Lord of all creation,*

Stir me up. Wake me up.
Give me a new heart.
Let me grow and bloom
and be joyful
in you!

Readings: Isaiah 65:17–21; Psalms 30; John 4:43–54

Monday, March 10

In the book *In Water and in Blood*, Robert Schreiter presents the biblical symbols of water and blood as signs of life and signs of death. Water runs through today's readings as a source of life and healing.

It is Ezekiel, the visionary, that we meet in the first reading. Water flowing from the temple is a symbol for God, the source of all life. This image of water reflecting the power and presence of God is found elsewhere in the Bible, but Ezekiel's vision is mirrored in a special way in Revelation 22.

Psalm 46 is a prayer of confidence in God (the inspiration for Martin Luther's hymn, "A Mighty Fortress Is Our God"). The river flowing through the city of God, Jerusalem, is a symbol of God's presence, power, and protection.

The healing miracle in John takes place at the side of the pool, but the man is healed by Christ's word, not by water. Perhaps the proximity of the pool communicates, one more time, that God's presence, power, and protection dwell among us in Jesus Christ.

O God, may the sight of water cure our blindness that we may grow in recognition of your presence among us.

Readings: Ezekiel 47:1–9, 12; Psalms 46; John 5:1–16

The hour is coming, and now is here, when the dead will hear the voice of the Son of God, and those who hear will live.

—John 5:25

Jesus, send us to rise
to the moment that is already,
to the sound of come out,
to the call show yourselves
shining and fearless.

But, Jesus, send us to rise
slowly, for shrouds of snow peeled back
from mountain trails like ripped skin
expose us. Winds whip, sting like angry life,
and our proud selves don't dare cry—instead
pull in tight, doubt in the numbness
of fingers, in the weakness of legs
that must get up and walk
this daily highway of promise and risk.

Jesus, send us to rise again to life,
getting practice for resurrection.

Perhaps today would be a good day to go outside and see how there are signs of Easter making themselves known, to look around me and see who are taking the risks of being identified as Christians, to be a witness myself!

Readings: **Isaiah 49:8–15; Psalms 145; John 5:17–30**

Wednesday, March 12

Remember me, O LORD, when you show favor to your people. —Psalms 106:4

We pray these words confidently because we have experienced God's unconditional love, as did those whom Moses was leading out of the land of Egypt. Unfortunately we, like them, often turn aside from God's way and forget God's promises. Are we also, then, a "stiff-necked people"? Do we substitute "golden calves" for God? Do we really believe in Jesus, the one God has sent? Do we put our belief into action and live according to his gospel message?

This Lenten season gives us an opportunity to pray more intensely and to reflect on our choices and values. Jesus reproached the people for not believing in him, the one sent by God, and for not having the love of God within them. We pray that our faith be strengthened—not only that we remember God's loving actions over the centuries and in our own lives but that our faith be deepened and our hearts be more receptive to God's faithful love.

Today I will take time to step aside from my busyness, to quiet down and open myself to God's word.

Readings: **Exodus 32:7–14; Psalms 106; John 5:31–47**

Today's readings aren't easy ones. They speak of wickedness, of blindness, of secret; they get to the heart of the matter. The purpose for which Jesus took on our humanity is coming closer. His life is about to be put on the line. Jesus is going up to Jerusalem.

Often my life is not easy; I may be tempted to wickedness, to blindness, to secret. I may be tempted to avoid the heart of the matter—to avoid those events that are of the utmost importance to my Christian way of life. How do I respond then? Do I give in? Do I turn away rather than "go up to Jerusalem."

Psalm 34:4 consoles us:
"I sought the Lord, and he answered me, and delivered me from all my fears."

Jesus prayed these words of the psalmist often. They enabled him to say, "The one who sent me is true." He was empowered to do the hard tasks, to speak openly, to go it alone, to do whatever he was called to do while he waited for his hour to come.

Readings: Wisdom 2:1a, 12–22; Psalms 34; John 7:1–2, 10, 25–30

Surely you are not also from Galilee, are you? Search and you will see that no prophet is to arise from Galilee. —John 7:52

We read the above and immediately condemn the Pharisees for making such a statement—judging a person according to where he lives. But are we not guilty of the same kind of judgments at times?

Two thousand years later, we still hear similar statements—"How can you trust that fellow? Don't you know he comes from the south side of town?" Or, "How can a woman with her background teach religion?" And, "How can you listen to a talk on spirituality by that man? He only has a high school education!"

How often we judge people by where they live, the type of clothes they wear, or the color of their skin. Nicodemus tells us that we cannot condemn a man without listening to him and finding out what he does.

All-knowing God, help me today to practice the words of Nicodemus and judge all I meet as I wish to be judged—by what I say and do.

Readings: Jeremiah 11:18–20; Psalms 7; John 7:40–53

No longer shall they teach one another, or say to each other, "Know the LORD," for they shall all know me, from the least of them to the greatest, says the LORD. —Jeremiah 31:34

The church chooses a most encouraging Old Testament passage for our reflection as we approach the holiest days of the year. Jeremiah has struggled for years to bring God's people to repentance, but they have persistently turned away from God's faithfulness.

Out of this dismal past, Jeremiah begins to speak of a new covenant in the future that will bring with it the forgiveness of all their sins. We who have inherited life in Christ, the New Covenant, have experienced that loving forgiveness too. Yet, forgiving others is also a part of this covenant. How I take this all for granted! There are even Christian groups that cannot live in peace, having built a climate of competition or revenge.

In these last days of Lent, I will dwell gratefully on the forgiveness that Jesus brings by his dying and rising and ask for strength for myself and all those who desire peace but find it difficult to forgive.

March 16, Fifth Sunday of Lent

Readings: Jeremiah 31:31–34; Psalms 51; Hebrews 5:7–9; John 12:20–33

He…said to them, "Let anyone among you who is without sin be the first to throw a stone at her."…Jesus was left alone with the woman standing before him.   —John 8:7, 9

Alone with you, Lord, the stones put down, I feel safe enough to admit that I am both the accuser and the accused. Self-righteous at times, I judge those who do not measure up to my standards or expectations. Yet in moments of weakness, I turn my back on my own commitments, thinking only of pleasure and comfort. Readily poised to strike out or defend myself, my heart carries the weight and hardness of stones.

But you, Lord, bend down and gently touch the earth, our common ground. Hands that bless, not strike or defend, can caress the soft texture of the dirt and heal hearts that are heavy and hard.

Help me to name the stones I have been throwing or dodging and reduce them to fertile earth this Lent.

Readings: Deuteronomy 13:1–9, 15–17, 19–30; Psalms 23; John 8:1–11

In good faith, the Israelites left Egypt and set out for the Promised Land. But, wandering in the wilderness of Sinai, they missed the meager comforts of life in Egypt. They longed to return to the security they once had—even if this meant a return to slavery.

On this journey, poisonous snakes attack and kill many of them. Only then do they realize their sin and ask God for forgiveness. God hears their prayer and offers salvation in a most unusual way—if the Israelites who have been poisoned gaze on the image of a snake mounted on a pole, they will be saved.

Are we very different from these people of long ago? Didn't we embrace our Lenten journey with enthusiasm, convinced that this would be a wonderful opportunity to grow in the spiritual life? Now, five weeks into Lent, the pinch of self-denial is sharp. We are tempted to abandon our Lenten commitments and return to a life of comfort and mediocrity. But, like those ancient wanderers, we are invited to look to Jesus, the sinless one, who was lifted high on a cross. In him we can come to salvation and fullness of life.

O God of life, God of surprises, free me from my enslavements and earthly securities. May I continue my Lenten journey with Jesus to Calvary—to hear the joy and delight of that awesome message: He is risen!

Readings: **Numbers 21:4–9; Psalms 102; John 8:21–30**

Are you the one to build me a house to live in?
—2 Samuel 7:5

Kneading and smoothing the wood, Joseph contemplates the words of scripture. They have new meaning as life has taken a turn toward the unknown—this woman is with child. Joseph, spirit moved to anticipation of unfolding discovery, is silent and watches, waiting and wondering. Scents of olive and sandalwood permeate his workshop as his thoughts jump to scenes of his own childhood, and he muses on a child who will bear his fathering mark of work, love, and play.

The master craftsman alone in his decisions watches the wood come to life under his hands. The crafter and the craft become one. We too wait for answers in our lives as we journey each day. We rub the wood with hands and heart and see the grain emerge in a mirrored finish.

Joseph, I come to you with the wood shavings of my life. Help me reshape, polish, and bring to life the gifts our God has given me—my life, which is still in progress. Help me to clean and polish one area of this life today.

Readings: **2 Samuel 7:4–5a, 12–14a, 16; Psalms 89; Romans 4:13, 16–18, 22; Matthew 1:16, 18–21, 24a**

O give thanks to the LORD, call on his name, make known his deeds among the peoples.

—Psalms 105:1

During the season of Lent, the idea of thanking God takes a back seat in our readings. In one of the prayers for the liturgy, though, we are urged to "show our thanks to God by performing acts of self-denial."

In a world where we are constantly encouraged to put our wants and desires first, we sometimes forget the nobility of an act of self-denial. Giving up sweets or denying ourselves our favorite television show are just some of the ways we can sacrifice for the Lord. At times even more of a sacrifice is the act that gives pleasure to others or relieves their discomfort. Words of kindness spoken to an outsider or stranger and the reassuring hug or pat on the back to someone who is insecure are Lenten practices filled with the love of God.

Jesus Christ bids us to take up our cross and follow him. The rewards that are to come happen as we make our way and give him thanks.

Jesus, help me to see the needs of others, to understand that my gifts are to be shared. Let me be strengthened in my ability to lighten the load of those who walk with me on the way. Then, my cross can become my gift of thanks to you.

Readings: Genesis 17:3–9; Psalms 105; John 8:51–59

On a recent television show that focused on capital punishment, a lawyer involved in one of the featured cases was interviewed. In the interview he spoke of an intense period of prayer that led him to believe that God was "on his side." This convinced him that the death penalty was called for in this case.

Most of life's problems cannot be reduced to two sides. We cannot draw a chalk line in the street and then choose sides, as we did as children. Many problems and situations are multifaceted. A piece of the truth can often be found in each facet.

Instead of taking sides we are called, like Jeremiah, to entrust our case to God. Our God, who "probes mind and heart," will lead us to the truth. Then we can confidently claim, not that God is on our side, but rather that "the LORD is with me, like a mighty champion" (Jeremiah 10:11, NAB).

God of truth, expand the boundary lines of my mind and heart. Help me to seek the truth wherever it may be found, even in some unlikely nooks and crannies of life.

Readings: Jeremiah 20:10–13; Psalms 18; John 10:31–42

Tomorrow is Passion Sunday! Where did the time go?

We are on the doorstep of Holy Week. Let us pause, reflect, and evaluate our progress toward change and growth this Lent. There are so many distractions in today's world that continually pull us away from our goal. Perhaps we struggled and stumbled along as each day presented its challenge. Yet, we continue for we know he "will deliver us from our sins" (Ezekiel 37:23), and we will come to "a covenant peace with our God" (Ezekiel 37:26).

The scripture readings on this eve of Passion Sunday are so rich in hope and encouragement. They call us to come into an awe-filled time of prayer, so steeped in love. Each verse has its own invitation.

I will take a few extra minutes today to reflect on these readings and select one verse that speaks to me in a special way. I will say it often during this day so that I, like the psalmist, may

Be strong, and let your heart take courage, all you who wait for the Lord. (Psalms 31:24)

Readings: **Ezekiel 37:21–28; Psalms 31; John 11:45–56**

> I did not hide my face from insult and spitting.
> —Isaiah 50:6

What better way to begin this week we call *holy*, this week in which we are invited to contemplate the passion of Jesus, than by taking up the crosses, the very real burdens, of our own lives and walking through these days with Jesus?

We are not invited to do this by following from afar, only listening to stories retold. Rather, we are invited to make the journey through this week—as through our lives—like Jesus, shouldering our burdens, our crosses, for and with others.

We are invited to do this willingly, simply, uncomplainingly for the poor, for our despondent next-door neighbor, for those struggling with evil in their lives, for our own loved ones. We are invited to do this in such a way that, by grace and sensitivity, we lighten rather than add to the burdens of others.

> What weighs me down at this moment in my life?
> How can I take up this cross in such a way as to lighten the burden of someone else?

Readings: Mark 11:1–10; Isaiah 50:4–7; Psalms 22; Philippians 2:6–11; Mark 15:1–39

Gentle me, Lord,
I, a bruised reed about to break.
Strength! That's what I need from you.
Your strength—your healing hands to whole me—
Your breath upon my spirit—Gentle,
Not to extinguish but to light me back to Life.

You know all about reeds.
Reeds that bend and break with slashings
And with mock homage.
About Life-light dimming to darkness
On the crude wood.
Lord, bruised and broken for me,
Life-quenched for me,
Dying that I might live.
Lord, in these most holy days,
Let your suffering, your death light the world
And be its resurrection.

Remind me daily, Lord, that bruised reeds and
flickering candles are all about me. I can offer not
what you offer—light and life—but just a little that
costs me nothing: a soft word, an encouraging smile,
an attentive ear—in memory of You.

Readings: Isaiah 42:1–7; Psalms 27;
John 12:1–11

I will give you as a light to the nations, that my salvation may reach to the end of the earth.
—Isaiah 49:6

What does it mean to be as *"a light to the nations"*? In the readings for today, Jesus calls his disciples to be that light. Judas and Peter responded in quite different ways.

Judas could not see how they could be a light if they did not have enough money to take care of their own needs. Confidence that God would be with them in whatever they did for others was missing. Had he not heard Jesus speak about the birds of the air and the lilies of the field?

Peter, always the sure one, loved Jesus. He was ready to die with him. He always meant well but fell into the trap of *self*-reliance. He came apart in fear when confronted by the servant in the courtyard. He too forgot the care that Jesus had promised them.

Where am I on this continuum? Probably somewhere in between. Has this Lent made a difference in my relationship with the Lord, or am I still in the same old pattern of life? It is not too late to make a difference, especially during these days of Holy Week. What activities can I put aside to spend more time in prayerful consideration of what I am doing with my time and my life? How can I make these next few days a turning point?

Readings: Isaiah 49:1–6; Psalms 71; John 3:21–33, 36–38

Today's readings offer us models of how the gift of speech can be used to build up or to destroy. The first reading from the prophet Isaiah provides us with words attributed to the suffering servant—a prefiguration of Christ. The psalmist (Psalm 50) carries a premessianic message as well. Both of these Old Testament writers point the way to Jesus, who will come as the sacrificial Lamb, quietly bearing humiliation, rejection, and violence at the hands of those he came to serve.

We can feel the pain behind the words of these Old Testament people. We can feel the pain and sadness in the words of Jesus in the gospel as he confronts Judas—whose words bartered away the life and mission of Jesus for thirty pieces of silver.

Will our words today bring about healing or hurt?
Will our words build up or destroy?
Will our words remind people of Jesus or Judas?

Lord, you have given me a well-trained tongue. Help me use it to speak words of truth and love to build up your kingdom.

Readings: Isaiah 50:4–9a; Psalms 69; Matthew 26:14–25

Jesus answered [Peter], "Unless I wash you, you have no share with me. ...I have set you an example, that you also should do as I have done to you."
—John 13:8, 15

This is my body....This...is...my blood....Do this...in remembrance of me.
— 1 Corinthians 11:24, 25

Jesus is ready to wash all humanity clean, to save all people of all time. Not with ordinary water does he wash us, but with his most precious blood and water from his side. He pours out his very life for all...for me.

Today we place ourselves before our Savior, deeply aware that he loves us even in our sin. We allow ourselves to be made new by the outpouring of this sacred blood and water. We feel its warm and cleansing power freeing us from all that would separate us from God.

What shall I return to the Lord for all his bounty to me (Psalms 116)? On this Holy Thursday Jesus speaks the response he desires, "Love one another as I have loved you" (John 15:12).

I will spend some time in quiet with Jesus and ask him to show me *who* and *how* to love. What grace do I need to make my return of love? Jesus assures me today that I will find it in the eating of his body and the drinking of his blood.

Readings: Exodus 12:1–8, 11–14; Psalms 116; 1 Corinthians 11:23–26; John 13:1–15

Blessed be the LORD, for he has wondrously shown his steadfast love to me.

—Psalms 31:21

The image of Jesus being lifted high on the cross is one filled with the awe of mystery, dignity, and respect. This is Jesus' "finest hour." He has surrendered all to God, the Father, giving body and soul, mind, will, and desire, keeping nothing but the face of love.

As we look up, immersed in sorrow at Jesus' pain and sufferings, Jesus gazes down upon us and the world of yesterday, tomorrow, and today. His eyes hold the deepest compassion for us, for all humankind, who cannot fathom so overwhelming a love.

O Jesus, your death on a cross is the link we have between heaven and earth, the bridge over which your love continuously crosses to us, yet is returned by so few.

Today, Jesus, help me to bypass the seeming ugliness of suffering and try to understand that all human beings are worthy of respect, full of mystery, and ever deserving of the dignity of their creation.

March 28, Good Friday

Readings: **Isaiah 52:13–53; Psalms 31; Hebrews 4:14–16, 5:7–9; John 18:1—19:42**

So shall my word be that goes out from my mouth; it shall not return to me empty, but it shall accomplish that which I purpose, and succeed in the thing for which I sent it.

—Isaiah 55:11

The word of God is life-giving. It is vibrant and powerful. It is a word of promise, a word that can be trusted. It is a faithful word.

"Do not be alarmed....He has been raised....You will see him, just as he told you" (Mark 16:6–7). This message is given to the women. Jesus is risen! The Word of God, made flesh, has carried out the will of the Father and has succeeded in what he was sent to do.

We have been given Jesus. The Word of God lives among us. Filled with new life, we are sent to proclaim the Risen One. We are church! We are Easter people! It is within the community of believers, the people of God, that his saving work becomes a reality.

Let us not seek him in faraway places or in times past. Jesus walks with us today! He is in our midst!

Thanks be to God!

Readings: **Genesis 1:1—2:2; Exodus 14:15—15:1; Isaiah 55:1–11; Psalms 42; Romans 6:3–11; Mark 16:1–8**

Isn't it curious that the very core of our Christian belief is based on a surface emptiness, an initial nothing! **"[John] also went in, and he saw and believed" (John 20:8)**—believed first in the word of Mary that Jesus was no longer where they had laid him, believed first that Jesus was not where they expected him to be.

This first Sunday morning the friends of Jesus are confused, sorrowful, frightened, unsure of the future, at a loss to explain why they are still hanging around. Not faith in the resurrection but simple human love draws the women to the tomb to minister some signs of respect for the body of Jesus. They are doing what comes next in ordinary, everyday relationships of love and friendship.

We must remember when we get discouraged with ourselves that our faith is not complete, a tidy package all finished and tied up in enduring heavy-duty twine. Like John and Peter and Mary, we come to fullness of faith slowly as we do the ordinary, extraordinary acts of everyday life that human love and relationships require of us. More often faith in Jesus Christ is not a flash of decision; it is cumulative.

Risen Christ, raise my eyes to your presence in my life. Help me to look more deeply into our life together.

Readings: Acts 10:34a, 37–43; Psalms 118; Colossians 3:1–4; John 20:1–9

IN ORDER OF APPEARANCE:

Sisters Jean Young, Joan Wickers, Frances Carmela Wade, Regina Suplick, Ann Stango, Rosemary Smith, Maureen Shaughnessey, Frances Scarfone, Julie Scanlan, M. Madeleine Rose, Clare Mary Roden, Therese Aquinas Roche, Grace Reape, Francis Raftery, Kathleen Quigley, Jean Cordis Mangin, Anne McDonald, Bernadette T. McCann, Grace Roberta McBreen, Maureen Mylott, Catherine Morrisett, Judy Mertz, Roseann Mazzeo, Rose Marie Padovano, Therese Dorothy Leland, Maria Cordis Lamendola, Alberta Keuhlen, Ellen Joyce, Deborah Humphreys, Edna Francis Hersinger, Carol Heller, Marie Henry, Mary Heffernan, Cheryl France, Kathleen Flanagan, Mary Farrell, Mary Fallon, Ellen Dauwer, Mary Cullen, Barbara Connell, Francis Maria Cassidy, Ursula Carr, Mary Canavan, Ceil Burns, Audrey Boettcher, Francis Cordis Bernardo, Jean Whitley.

Artists:	Mary Culhane, S.C.
	Frances Scarfone, S.C.
Cover:	Anne Haarer, S.C.